MY GRANDMOTHER DIED AGAIN

& Other Almost Believable Excuses

Warren S. Blumenfeld, Ph.D.

Illustrated by Cal Warlick

PEACHTREE PUBLISHERS. LTD.

Atlanta

Published by
PEACHTREE PUBLISHERS, LTD.
494 Armour Circle, N.E.
Atlanta, Georgia 30324

Manufactured in the United States of America

10 9 8 7 6 5 4 3 2

Cover illustration by Cal Warlick
Interior design by Candace J. Magee

Library of Congress Cataloging in Publication Data

Blumenfeld, Warren S.
    My grandmother died again & other almost believable excuses /
Warren S Blumenfeld ; illustrated by Cal Warlick.
      p.   cm
   ISBN 1-56145-053-7 (trade paper) : $5.95
   1. Excuses—Humor.   I. Title. II. Title: My grandmother died
again and other almost believable excuses.
PN6231.E87B5   1991
818'.5402—dc20   90-28258
                                    CIP

To all grandmothers — past, present, and future — real and imagined — but especially to my grandmother Rebecca Blumenfeld and to my son's grandmother Fagel Blumenfeld, both of whom are now past, and both of whom were more real than you can imagine . . . and both of whom would have gotten such a kick out of all this.

And, as always, to my wife Esther and to our son Josh.

Other Books by Warren S. Blumenfeld, Ph.D.

JUMBO SHRIMP *& Other Almost Perfect Oxymorons:
Contradictory Expressions That Make Absolute Sense*

PRETTY UGLY: *More Oxymorons & Other Illogical Expressions That Make Absolute Sense*

CONTENTS

INTRODUCTION
If you live long enough, you'll hear everything

Dear Occupant:

At one time or another, *everyone* has said to himself or herself something along the lines of "I must have heard enough excuses to write a book."

Me too.

One nice thing about teaching — particularly university teaching— is you get to hear all kinds of neat excuses. (I forget what the other nice thing about teaching is.)

While it is often suggested if you live long enough, you'll hear everything, I seriously doubt it — but you will hear *enough*.

And not only have I heard enough, but when people — *and* colleagues and students — heard about my interest in collecting excuses, even more poured in until now I have become sort of a national excuse repository. (But more about that later.)

Why then this book? Read on.

Well, my short answer excuse for writing this book is:

(a) Word of my collection got around,

(b) I signed a contract, and

(c) My publisher won't let me out of it.

Actually, I had another excuse — a beauty — but the word processor ate it (and belched).

When Push Comes To Shove

Now — and this is important — *by excuses, I do NOT mean lies*. This book is *not* intended to be a liar's manual. There are already enough of those around — manuals *and* liars — and I do not plan to contribute to either category.

By excuses, I mean the kind of essentially innocent behavior we all (save you perfect people . . . both of you) exhibit when push comes to shove . . . when we are pushed and/or shoved into a corner.

For example, . . .

You finally screw up the courage to make that dental appointment you have been putting off for the last six (seven, tops) years — during which time the two-minute drill has been a concept restricted totally to professional football. On the drive to the dental office, you notice this strange ping in your engine you never *ever* noticed before (to say nothing about the slight wobble whenever you make a right turn). Naturally, you immediately head for the automobile dealership to have it checked. While you wait for an opinion (and an estimate), you call the dental office, explaining:

"I have to cancel my appointment; I suddenly developed car trouble."

Right.

On the other hand, such things *do* happen; and, if not corrected, they *can* take a terrible toll on your car.

Or . . .

You and your significant other are invited by your boss to attend a children's violin (beginners) recital which will include the boss's only, and extremely precocious, eight-year-old daughter — the one so fond of describing you as "the short chubby little man with the funny wig who has that easy job at my Daddy's office." The recital, conveniently scheduled for Super Bowl Sunday and located on the other side of town, is planned for three hours (four, tops), beginning at 2:00 p.m. She will play her two-minute duet "some time after 2:15."

At noon, as you shave on a Sunday for the first time in a long time, you get a call from your favorite uncle — the unmarried (and extremely wealthy) one with you in his will, away all these many years on an archaelogical dig — telling you not only is he at the airport between planes but he *must* see you . . . something about his will. Naturally you immediately call your boss; and . . .

Certainly.

On the other hand, . . .

Well, you get the idea (actually, you're probably way ahead of me already — but then, I have an excuse). We imperfect people do it all the time. Welcome to the club, albeit not a very exclusive club. And we all continue to pay our dues, several times over.

As a matter of fact, as you proceed through this book (and you *will*), you will not only recognize some excuses, but also some people — *most especially* (unless you are indeed perfect) *you*.

To Excuse Is Human

What we *all* are is *human* — and some of us are more human than others. And occasionally offering excuses is universal.

. . . and for that reason, from this point on, I am addressing *only* the imperfect among us. Perfect people can take the rest of the day and/or the book off — unless they have some excuse to stay with the rest of us.

Anything IS Possible

As a matter of fact, one of the few (mercifully) premises of this book is anything *is* possible. The most outrageous excuse (or if you prefer, explanation . . . or reason) just *could be* true.

Let me illustrate this anything is possible reality with a personal experience — one that not only makes the point, but also continues to embarrass me.

It Takes Two To Tangle

In my first quarter of teaching, when I thought students would try to take advantage of me (and when students would try to take advantage of me), I initiated, and held strictly to a no-cut (no unexcused absences) class attendance policy. I was serious; and I was taken seriously . . . seriously.

Anyway, came the midterm examination, two not-so-good, stretching-for-mediocrity, students (obviously buddies) failed to show up for class, minimally a capital offense even on a regular class day, and now compounded by the scheduled exam. A few hours after class, I received a phone call from one of the students. He informed me he had been in a five-car pileup on the interstate, had just finished satisfying the police and the insurance people, and could we work something out?

Sure.

"We'll see," I replied sagely.

Not more than ten minutes later, I received a call from the other student. He went through the *same* story, *verbatim, no* deviations, also concluding with the could we work something out ending.

Right.

Once again I replied sagely, "We'll see." (You think it's easy to be a sage?)

Could it be? Was it possible? What a coincidence! My statistician's instincts began to take over. Be still, my computer. The probability of such a dual occurrence was mind boggling!

Then, I called the police in the accident's jurisdiction for corroboration of the two accidents. The officer not only corroborated the two stories, but also informed me the two students were involved in the same five-car pileup on the interstate! (GASP!)

Two things *(at least)* came of the experience:

(1) We spent a great deal of class time that quarter talking about, and computing, probabilities; and

(2) (and more important, at least in terms of this book) I have never, *ever*, again doubted an excuse . . . because anything *is* possible.

. . . but I do allow some explanations do more for the upward mobility of my eyebrows than others.

My Grandmother Died Again *(Sound Familiar?)*

Some excuses are indeed institutionalized. Consider the accepted tradition of the massive passing away of grandmothers everywhere in the United States each year on opening day of the baseball season (except here in in Atlanta, where, all too sadly enough, Braves baseball is admittedly an oxymoron).

And maybe they *do* pass away; but it's highly unlikely. Unlikely yes, but it does sorta bring me to the title of this book. (I told you it sounded familiar.)

Several years ago, I had a student who missed class early in the quarter because his grandmother passed away. Obviously, it does happen . . . to all of us. The student naturally went to the funeral. Just before the end of the quarter, the student again missed class. Upon his return, he reported, **"My grandmother died again."**

His grief was real . . . and obvious. Even an insensitive person like me could see it. My sudden and unprecedented burst of sensitivity notwithstanding, it was all I could do not to laugh— or at least smile. As you certainly have already figured out, he had lost both his maternal and his paternal grandmothers in a relatively short period of time — which was tragic.

It was his report that was comic.

Ergo, MY GRANDMOTHER DIED AGAIN.

EDUCATION
The dog ate it, but . . .

Excuse me if I begin with an education episode, but education is where I've been moving the knowledge frontier for the past twenty-three plus years . . . although I won't indicate in which direction. But that's another story — and another book.

Ergo (he said academically), let me share a few of my favorites.

A not too good, but apparently well-meaning, student of mine failed to turn in his term paper on time. The apparently good, but not too well-meaning, excuse offered was:

"The dog ate it; *(pause)* **but if you can wait an hour, I can get it back for you."**

Right.

What do you think?

Me too. Not unlike (or perhaps like) the presumed dog, I naturally passed. Hey, I'm smarter than I look.

But I do think the excuse showed some imagination — as well as some cheek. (It also might make a nice title for an episode in a book.)

As a matter of fact, it is uncanny how often "The dog ate it" turns up when term papers do not. It apparently is a universal phenomenon . . . packs of marauding dogs roaming campuses devouring all term papers in their path.

THE DOG ATE IT

On that score, I have it on reasonably good authority, at another university, when an instructor had finally had it with that particular excuse, she challenged the student with, "I happen to know you don't happen to have a dog" — to which the quick-thinking student replied, "That's OK; I didn't happen to have a term paper either."

Gotcha!

It's difficult to argue with logic like that. Presumably, they called it a draw.

Once, however, I was involved in one of those rare occasions where the instructor's logic did prevail over the student's sorta logic. An undergraduate — as I recall, a senior with a sophomore's perspective on life — eased into class about an hour late. When I later called him on it, he replied:

"I forgot about the time change; and I didn't reset my watch."

Good enough. . . except it was February.

I am indebted to a former colleague for what might be referred to as the *nouveau riche* excuse.

Many years ago, a student failed to show up for class. The telephone rang (as it always seems to); and the no-show relayed the following message:

"I wasn't in class today because our son fell and hit his head on the color television set."

And while I suppose the late Walt Disney and/or the plucky, but plucked, NBC peacock would be pleased as punch and proud as a whatever, it didn't do much for my colleague — except to give him a good excuse to share with me . . . and now with you.

More recently, another colleague told me of one of his graduate students who, after failing to make an evening deadline for a term paper, slipped the term paper under the professor's door some time in the pre-dawn hours before the start of the next school day with the following explanation:

"I'm sorry to be late with this term paper, but my wife had our baby last night. I promise it won't happen again this quarter."

And, to the best of my knowledge, it did *not* happen again that quarter — thereby giving the offending student at least a modicum of credibility. Had it happened again that quarter, there can be little doubt I would be writing this — and you would be reading this — in either *The New England Journal of Medicine* and/or *The Guinness Book of World Records* rather than here.

OK then, buckle up (and keep your hands in the book) . . . and hang on to your eyebrows, your cynicism, your common sense, your compassion, your sense of reality, and your sense of humor — but not necessarily in that order. Here we go, taking that excusable insightful slippery slope slide.

What Are You Gonna Say?

ATTENTION, STUDENTS — you find yourself in the following sticky situation:

You are a student in a senior level university class in which a term paper was assigned on the first day of class and is due on the last day of class. The last day of class comes (as it always does, mercifully — regardless of which side of the desk you spend your waking, or other, hours). For whatever reason (hey, that's *your* problem — and that's what this book is all about), you have no term paper to turn in.

OK; potentially perpetually perennially paperless person (and would-be excuse scholar), you're up. **What are you gonna say?** Try one (or more) of the following tried (and maybe true) explanations and/or excuses:

- ☐ "My typist let me down."
- ☐ "Thieves stole it."
- ☐ "Thieves stole it . . . last night."
- ☐ "The photocopier chewed it up."
- ☐ "It was so good I already submitted it for publication. "
- ☐ "I thought it was due *next* week."
- ☐ "It's in my husband's briefcase . . . on its way to (city *at least* 500 miles away)."
- ☐ "I was up all night with a sick child."
- ☐ "I was up all night with a sick thief."
- ☐ "My grandmother died again."
- ☐ "It's in my locked car; and my wife lost the keys."
- ☐ "It was destroyed in the fire."
- ☐ "The dog ate it."
- ☐ "My parents were so proud of it they kept it to show their friends."
- ☐ "It's still at the bindery."
- ☐ "My co-author has it . . . and a broken leg."
- ☐ "I spilled coffee on the only copy this morning."
- ☐ "I must have lost it between the parking lot and here."
- ☐ "My son took it to SHOW & TELL."
- ☐ "It accidentally got thrown out with the rest of the garbage."

Try the following on for sighs.

The 1988 Democratic Convention was here in Atlanta. Traffic was predictably unpredictable. One particular student, with minimal credibility (and with the attention span of a flash bulb), was consistently late for class. On one such occasion, she volunteered she had been caught in a convention parade.

Reasonable enough — except the convention had concluded the week before.

It turned out the student was no better in class than she was in (not so) current events.

The mind — at least mine — begins to boggle when one considers the opportunities the 1996 Summer Olympic Games here in Atlanta will afford the creative student . . . to say almost nothing of the creative instructor (and other locals). Excusing may indeed be added to the list of competitive events. If so, I anticipate a player-coach role.

Let's move on, giving equal time to excuses proffered by professors (not all of whom are as perfect as either of us would like).

How about taking an objective look at the other side of the student/faculty coin? How about those times when the excuses are flowing profusely from the other side of the desk? Can faculty be as creative as students? After all, we have more experience — and wonderfully relevant experience at that.

In a word (or three), Yes we can . . . and just as often.

For example, consider the instructor who, when asked by an appropriately hostile class why the promised exams were not yet graded, replied :

"I was called in unexpectedly by the Pentagon to consult on a problem!"

. . . and got away with it!

ATTENTION, FACULTY — you find yourself in the following sticky situation:
You are the instructor in a graduate level university course. After having done your

opening day Cotton Mather imitation regarding the evils of being late to class, you arrive twelve minutes (fifteen minutes, according to some of the more testy — and secure — students) late to class.

OK; Mr. — or Ms. — Chips, you terribly tardy taut teacher, you're up. **What are you gonna say?**

☐ "I was held hostage in a bank robbery."
☐ "I was counseling a student and lost track of time."
☐ "The elevator service in this building is terrible."
☐ "I was writing recommendations for a student."
☐ "I was helping a colleague with a manuscript."
☐ "I stopped to help a student give birth."
☐ "My grandmother died again."
☐ "There was some sort of student demonstration."
☐ "I was giving a phone interview to a radio station."
☐ "My watch must have stopped."
☐ "I thought we agreed on a later starting time."
☐ "I got caught in a parade."
☐ "The president of the university wanted to talk."
☐ "The clocks in this building are notoriously fast."

The question is often asked of me, "What do you do when a test is compromised . . . stolen?" Good question; the answer is simple.

I merely change the correct answers to the questions.

Works every time!

I STOPPED TO HELP A STUDENT GIVE BIRTH

Now how about things students tell parents?

ATTENTION, STUDENTS — you find yourself in the following sticky situation:

You are not really terribly enthusiastic about your second shot at seventh grade algebra. Unfortunately, with the possible exception of your teacher, no one is as excited about — or as interested in — you and that class as are your parents. Your midterm grades come in; and you have a real stranglehold on an absolute cinch D — with an outside chance at an F . . . *if* you apply yourself.

OK; my mighty mutant math major, you're up. ***What are you gonna say?***

☐ "Algebra is a dead language anyway."

☐ "I have a bad seat in class."

☐ "My typist let me down."

☐ "The teacher doesn't like me."

☐ "It's right after lunch; and it's hard to concentrate."

☐ "It's too cold in the room."

☐ "My grandmother died again."

☐ "It's too hot in the room."

☐ "I don't need algebra; I'm going to be a rock star when I grow up."

☐ "Someone stole my textbook."

☐ "Someone stole my textbook — several weeks ago."

☐ "My sweater is too tight."

☐ "I'm sitting too close to the front of the room."

☐ "My pencil broke."

. . . which brings us to the explanations parents give administrators.

I HAVE A BAD SEAT IN CLASS

ATTENTION, PARENTS — you find yourself in the following sticky situation:

You are a member of your children's school's PTA — not a terribly active member, but active enough that you can face your children with a relatively clear conscience (yours — not theirs).

One night at a PTA meeting, the president asks you, in front of the full membership, to coordinate the annual combination spaghetti dinner, talent show, garage sale, car wash, paper drive, and bake sale event (the true high point of the academic year) — indicating it shouldn't require more than four (five, tops) hours a day (including Sundays, during the NFL season) for the next few months.

OK; perversely perky potential PTA parent of the year, you're up. **What are you gonna say?**

☐ "We're going to be out of town."

☐ "We're going to be out of the country."

☐ "I have a bad back."

☐ "We did it three years ago . . . before you came."

☐ "This is going to be a very busy year for us."

☐ "My grandmother died again."

☐ "Our elderly parents will be moving in with us."

☐ "We will be on an around the world cruise."

☐ "We're considering moving."

☐ "We will be renovating the house."

☐ "We're expecting."

☐ "There are some personal problems that we can't discuss with you that will make it impossible."

11

Announced Pop Quiz (All Things Being EQ)

OK, the time has come to attempt to begin to measure your EQ. Yes, I said EQ, as in . . . And yes, perhaps not unlike you, I can't believe I wrote, or said, that.

Not so incidentally, you don't *have* to participate in this quiz (or the one that follows it, for that matter). However, if you opt not to participate, I'd like to know why not.

Anyway, your terribly testy task is to **select the most appropriate excuse for each sticky situation.**

. . . and no cheating, because if you're caught, you'll have to explain, and . . .

1. You are obviously sleeping in class. When asked why you are sleeping, what is your reply?
   - a. It's a learning technique often used in Eastern cultures.
   - b. I come from a long line of narcoleptics.
   - c. This is a note-taking technique the Learning Center taught me.
   - d. I was up all night making a friend sick.

2. You are an instructor obviously unprepared for class. When asked by the Dean why you are unprepared, what is your reply?
   - a. I had anticipated being on sabbatical leave this year.
   - b. I dropped my notes . . . and they broke.
   - c. Socrates misled us all; but the drinks are on me.
   - d. I believe in spontaneity; and this is the time and place for it.

3. You are in tenth grade; and your grades are falling faster than the temperature in North Dakota in November. When asked why by your parents, what is your reply?
   - a. I'm concentrating too much on one course.
   - b. I think I'm in love . . . again.
   - c. Everybody's grades have fallen.
   - d. It must be a computer glitch.

4. You are asked by the high school your children attend to monitor the cafeteria during lunch hours. What is your reply?
   a. My spouse and I are taking a course in advanced basket weaving at that time.
   b. My physician told me to stay away from stressful situations.
   c. I'm on a diet; and I don't think I could resist the temptation to partake.
   d. Broccoli gives me and President Bush gas.

Scoring Directions

This is the honor system. The correct answers are on page 89. Score yourself (if you are into that sort of thing). No cheating, and certainly no peeking.

Interpreting Your Score

Here are some normative guidelines.

Your Score	Excuse Level	Educational Equivalency	Pizza Equivalency
0	A	High School	Plain / Small
1	B	College	Deluxe / Medium
2	C	Graduate School	Super / Large
3	D	Post Graduate School	Supreme / Huge
4	E	Professional Activity	Ultimate / Gross

When The Time Is Right (Got A Match?)

OK (and even if it's not), as your EQ is measured, your ego is stroked, and your excusable thirst is slaked (I like that kind of talk!), what follows is a matching exercise.

Your terrifically testy task is to **match each sticky situation with the most appropriate excuse.**   Consider using the spaces provided for that happy task.

. . . and please hold the cheating to a minimum, because, once again, if you're caught (and yes, I *am* watching), you'll have to explain, and . . .

Sticky Situations

__A. You are an instructor who doesn't know the material.   A sharp student asks a question you cannot possibly answer.   What is your response to this stimulus?

__B. Your only child, a fourteen-year-old daughter, asks your permission to go on this six-month hitchhiking tour of the United States with a group of her friends (and a local rock group) rather than return to school in the fall.   When you say no, she asks why.

__C. On the day of the final (for which you are almost prepared), you walk in to the scheduled two-hour period with but fourteen minutes remaining.   The instructor asks you why.

__D. You are the Superintendent of Schools.   You are asked why you spent 85 percent of your budget on building improvements made by your brother-in-law's company.

__E. After your sixteen-year old son's series of failing grades, you are asked to come to school for a seven-week (daily) program of three-way conferences among teachers, students, and parents.   Your carefully considered response?

Appropriate Excuses

___ 1. Unfortunately, my textbook and notes were all destroyed in the flood following the most recent tidal wave.

___ 2. I didn't realize he was my brother-in-law.

___ 3. It is my understanding I have been scheduled for jury duty at any moment.

___ 4. We would like to share the joy of the new television season with you.

___ 5. Along with several others (who were released quickly), I was held as a hostage in a bank robbery.

Scoring Directions

Again, the correct answers are on page 89. Again, score yourself (if you are *still* into that sort of self-abuse). No cheating, and certainly no peeking.

Interpreting Your Score

Again, here are some normative guidelines.

Your Score	Interpretation of Your Score
0	Definitely should not be left at home alone under any circumstances.
1	May be left at home alone, but only for short periods of time.
2	May leave home, but should not attempt to cross streets alone.
3	May cross streets alone . . . but only with lights . . . and at corners.
4	May cross streets alone, with or without lights . . . anywhere on the block . . . . may go anywhere.
5	Not only may go anywhere, but is capable of working behind counter at a dry cleaning establishment.

Did I *not* include your favorite education-related excuse or sticky situation?

Not to worry, kindly and/or gently grasp word processor between thumb and forefinger, and let me hear about it. But whether kindly or gently, please do use the EXCUSE-O-GRAM so generously provided for that purpose on page 80.

The congenial Institute staff is always on the lookout for excellent excuses and/or sticky situations. Besides, when the next one of these excuses books comes out, the staff and I would be pleased to give *you* appropriate credit for your excusable insights (or incites, as the case may be).

Therefore, please be sure to spell your name correctly. (I suggest you check your driver's license, unless it has expired. And if it has expired, one might but wonder why.)

On the other hand, if there really *is* a reason why you can't contribute an excuse, I understand.

Sure.

However, it is important you understand I can't always take personal responsibility for receipt of your contributed excuse and/or sticky situation because a lot of mail has gotten lost lately . . . in the mail.

Y'all write, right? Do do **the write thing** (or you will indeed be in the wrong — and to wrong does not make a write).

WORKPLACE
There is a fire engine blocking my driveway

Most of us work — or at least know someone who does . . . or did.

Regarding the latter contingency, I readily confess to knowing more than a few people who are, apparently, easing into retirement gradually — rather than waiting until the last second. On that score, I intend to deal with procrastination in this book . . . but not now . . . maybe later.

Anyway, unless you and your organization are most unusual, excuses should be in wild abundance this time of year. It promises to be a bumper crop — although why anyone would want to try to grow bumpers is beyond me.

OK then, as the activist said, let's do it.

What Are You Gonna Say?

Let's begin with what is probably the most common — some might even suggest crass — excuse situation in the work world. And that is, why you (not me!) can't come in to work today.

ATTENTION, EMPLOYEES — (not unlike generations of employees before, during, and after you) you find yourself in the following sticky situation:

You are supposed to be at work at 8:00 a.m. It's an extremely typical Monday morning — except it follows a triple overtime game that didn't end until just after 1:30 a.m. It's raining, hard. What is laughingly referred to as the freeway is doing its usual elongated parking lot imitation . . . extremely well. And if you could borrow a fire engine to block your driveway, you would. Obviously, you are not going to make it to work today.

However, you do need to phone in your regrets.

OK, you're up. *What are you gonna say?*

☐ "Thieves stole my clothes; I have nothing to wear."

☐ "The police have sealed off the neighborhood while they go door to door searching for that escaped criminal you probably heard about."

☐ "The street is flooded."

☐ "I have that bug that seems to be going around."

☐ "I am being held hostage; but I hope to be in tomorrow."

☐ "I have to take the dog to the vet."

☐ "I can't explain now; the police need to keep the phone line clear."

☐ "My grandmother died again."

☐ "My driveway is iced over."

☐ "There is a wild animal loose in the neighborhood."

☐ "My car won't start."

☐ "I have jury duty. "

☐ "I need to be available for an important call from the lottery people."

☐ "There is a fire engine blocking my driveway."

☐ "It's very complicated; but if you have seventy feet of rope, that would be a great help."

THERE IS A FIRE ENGINE BLOCKING MY DRIVEWAY

ATTENTION, EMPLOYEES — you find yourself in the following sticky situation:

You are responsible for the completion of a project report . . . assigned six months ago. The due date arrives; the project report does not. In no uncertain terms, your supervisor wants to know why not. Welcome to the club (as in club or be clubbed).

OK, presumably poor perpetually procrastinating projecteer, you're up again. **What are you gonna say?**

☐ "The computer is down."
☐ "The air conditioning went out."
☐ "My typist let me down."
☐ "It's all this nuclear testing."
☐ "Was *I* supposed to do this?"
☐ "I've been sick."
☐ "My grandmother died again."
☐ "The program didn't run."
☐ "There was an airline strike."
☐ "The heat went off."
☐ "There's been a lot of flu going around."
☐ "I thought that was *their* responsibility."
☐ "The computer center let me down . . . again."
☐ "We had houseguests from out of town."
☐ "The fax is in the mail."

MY TYPIST LET ME DOWN

THE COMPUTER'S DOWN

My educated guess is every major, and maybe minor, city has a bar either called "The Office" or "The Library" for no other reason than it gives some people the traditional — and seemingly plausible

"... **because I was working late at the office**" and/or "... **because I was working late at the library**" excuse.

... and not the worst reason in the world either!

Hardly anyone ever opens up a bar called "The Bar." Somehow (lawyers *possibly* excluded) I don't think "... **because I was working late at the bar**" would be anywhere near as effective. (But it might be worth a shot . . . or two . . . if we have time.)

Anyway, said dutiful drinker's dilemma notwithstanding, we had both establishments near our campus (we are a university located downtown). Unfortunately — or fortunately, depending on your perspective — " The Library" recently closed (I am told). I don't know who suffered more from that closing — the students or the faculty. But I do know library assignments have lost their popularity . . . as well as their credibility.

(Incidentally, Dear, I'll be a little late getting home from the office tonight because . . .)

Have you tried dealing with bureaucracies and/or customers lately? . . . and from which direction?

Me too. Does the following sound familiar?

ATTENTION, EMPLOYER (OR EMPLOYEE) — you find yourself in the following sticky situation:

You are the individual in your organization responsible for coordinating deliveries to customers. At 5:45 p.m., a really irate customer calls to find out where in the county (or thereabouts) her delivery is.

OK, calmly cool confident cooperative coordinator, you're up.

What are you gonna say?

- ☐ "The dog ate it."
- ☐ "Today?"
- ☐ "We have a new man on the job."
- ☐ "The computer is down."
- ☐ "There is a trucking strike."
- ☐ "We're running a little late."
- ☐ "It's on back order."
- ☐ "There has been an accident on the interstate."
- ☐ "That's not my department."
- ☐ "My grandmother died again."
- ☐ "There's a computer error; we show you for tomorrow."
- ☐ "The president's motorcade has caused traffic havoc."
- ☐ "The salesperson really doesn't understand the delivery system."
- ☐ "It turns out you are just beyond the delivery area."
- ☐ "A lot of the staff is out with the flu."
- ☐ "There is a computer programmer strike."
- ☐ "Your order is in the back of the truck."
- ☐ "Your order is in the front of the truck."

ATTENTION, CUSTOMER — you find yourself in the following sticky situation:

You have unexpectedly received what simply has to be the ugliest and most useless (but in poor taste) gift you have ever seen — and from "that person" you have intensely disliked since high school. Your spouse, supportive as always, suggests either you or the gift leave the house . . . forever (or longer — whichever comes first).

The garbage collection people will not accept it. (It's a matter of their professional ethics.) What to do?

Fortunately, just before re-gift-wrapping the gift and leaving it unattended on the front seat of your unlocked car in the highest crime neighborhood of your city, you notice the (whatever it is) came from the store in town that advertises the customer can "bring anything back — absolutely no questions asked."

You drive to the store, readily revising rapidity records in the process, and indicate to the return desk supervisor you are there to return the (whatever it is). Advertising claims to the contrary, the return desk supervisor absolutely asks you *why* you are returning it.

OK, really rancored raucous riled recipient, you're up again.

What are you gonna say?

- [ ] "It's the wrong color."
- [ ] "We already have one of these."
- [ ] "Our floor is not strong enough to support the weight of this."
- [ ] "Our lease prohibits this."
- [ ] "We're moving to a smaller house."
- [ ] "Neither of us will ever learn how to use it."
- [ ] "We're moving to a larger house."
- [ ] "We both work."
- [ ] "My grandmother died again."
- [ ] "It's the wrong size."
- [ ] "We don't think it is appropriate for our teenager."
- [ ] "We just can't keep up the payments."
- [ ] "We are vegetarians."
- [ ] "We're moving to a larger apartment."
- [ ] "We're moving to a smaller apartment."
- [ ] "We already have two of these."
- [ ] "Our cat is allergic to it."
- [ ] "My elderly parents are moving in with us."

IT'S THE WRONG COLOR

All Things Being EQ

OK, once again, your task is to **select the most appropriate excuse for each sticky situation.**

1. You are not coming in to the shop today. When the boss asks you why not, what is your reply?
   - a. That skin condition from all those years in the jungle has recurred.
   - b. We have unexpected guests from out of town . . . the South Pole.
   - c. I had a skiing accident.
   - d. I have to wait for the plumber . . . *and* the electrician.

2. You are the boss; and you have just turned down a request for a salary raise. When you are asked why, what is your reply?
   - a. My boss has frozen all salaries.
   - b. The federal government has some sort of prohibition on raises.
   - c. It's company policy.
   - d. We are being monitored very closely by the IRS.

3. You are six (eleven, tops) weeks late in paying your apartment rent. When your landlord asks you why, what is your reply?
   - a. The IRS lost my refund check in the mail.
   - b. The male mailman ran off with the female mailman . . . and the mail, man.
   - c. My (spouse) lost it on the way over to your office.
   - d. The police impounded it as evidence in a bank robbery.

4. You are a loyal, dedicated, and professional secretary. When the boss asks you, at 5:35 on a Friday afternoon preceding a holiday weekend, to stay late to type a 130-page report, what is your reply?
   - a. I have to get home to care for my elderly llama.
   - b. The delivery people are coming some time between now and (next work day).

c. I have non-refundable tickets on a cruise ship.
d. I'm expecting an emergency long distance phone call.

Scoring Instructions
Correct answers are presented on page 89. Score yourself (ouch!).

Interpreting Your Score
As before.

Got A Match?

As before, your task is to **match each sticky situation with the most appropriate excuse.** Again, use the spaces provided. OK, let's do it (or have a good reason why not).

Sticky Situations
___A. After being out sick for a few days, you return to work with a bad sunburn. The boss asks you why.

___B. The letter you just typed has an average of 2.4 typographical errors per sentence. You are asked why.

___C. Your manuscript is two weeks late (so far). Your editor asks you why. (Note: Extra credit for this one.)

___D. After extracting a promise from the mechanic that your car will be ready by noon, you show up at 5:00 p.m. He casually asks you why.

___E. The car you promised the customer would be ready by the end of the day isn't. The customer expresses a certain curiosity.

Appropriate Excuses

___1. We had a crisis at the office; and I was the only one who was qualified to handle it.

___2. The dog ate my word processor; (pause) but, if you can wait an hour, . . .

___3. The special component has to be special-ordered.

___4. I just can't get my mind off of the potential extinction of all those snail darters in Tennessee.

___5. I was helping my son prepare for a Boy Scout test in fire building when he made a terrible mistake.

Scoring Directions

Correct answers are on page 89.   Do it (to) yourself, please.
How did you do?

Interpreting Your Score

As before.

The Write Stuff

As before.

GOVERNMENT
and L A W   E N F O R C E M E N T
My heel got stuck in the gas pedal

Everyone should have at least one Auntie Mame — even Patrick Dennis. My Auntie Mame's name was Aunt Devera.

Her (and, therefore, our) adventures *could* fill a book— but, relax, not this one. Among her other strengths, she demonstrated grace under pressure and was incredibly cool in *all* circumstances (and she certainly seemed to get into all circumstances). And she was not below (or above) engaging in the excuse-making behavior of which we speak here .

One of my favorite Aunt Devera stories (at least one I can repeat) concerns an automobile mishap in which she was involved — and happily one in which no one was hurt.

Aunt Devera's car was parked outside a shoe store . . . pointed at the shoe store. We'll never know for sure what happened. She claimed she put the car in Reverse — when indeed she put it in Drive.

And drive it did.

Away went Aunt Devera and the car, right through the store's front window (in the process creating perhaps the first drive-thru shoe store), sending assorted sling pumps, high heels, flats, and what have you — not to mention assorted not too amused customers and clerks — flying in all directions.

When the car finally came to a halt (helped considerably by the back wall of the store), the store manager rushed up to ask what had happened. Aunt Devera, without missing a beat, shot back:

"My heel got stuck in the gas pedal . . . and what do you have in a black pump? Size 6-1/2 B . . . preferably without too much of a heel."

Moving right along, if the following sticky situation does not sound familiar, you have indeed lived a sheltered life.

ATTENTION, CITIZENS WITH LICENSE TO DRIVE — you find yourself in the following sticky situation:

You are driving your brand new flame red imported sports car, studying the owner's manual, playing with all the automotive avionics, checking yourself in the mirror, listening to tapes (at the maximum), and hoping to see — or rather, to be seen by — your friends. In fact, you are paying attention to everything except the speed limit . . . and that funny little flashing blue light on that funny big white car behind you . . . closing rapidly.

The driver of said funny big white car with said funny little flashing blue light casually inquires as to why you were doing 40 MPH in a 25 MPH zone.

OK, summarily suspected suffering systematic speeder, you're up yet once again. *What are you gonna say?*

THERE WAS A BEE IN MY CAR

- ☐ "I was rushing to be on time for my appointment with the mayor."
- ☐ "My speedometer must be broken."
- ☐ "There was a bee in the car."
- ☐ "I'm not used to an automatic transmission."
- ☐ "I was running out of gas."
- ☐ "I'm a college professor . . . late for a final."
- ☐ "My grandmother died again."
- ☐ "My pet snake got loose; and I was distracted."
- ☐ "I'm sunburned."
- ☐ "I had to go to the bathroom . . . *bad.*"
- ☐ "My heel got stuck in the gas pedal."
- ☐ "What speed limit sign?"
- ☐ "Certainly you know speed limit is an oxymoron."
- ☐ "I'm late for the babysitter."
- ☐ "I'm trying to get home in time to watch the Braves game."

ATTENTION, POTENTIALLY RE-ELECTABLE INCUMBENT CANDIDATES — you find yourself in the following sticky situation:

After one term in office as county commissioner, you are running for re-election. Your entire campaign is built around the theme of "thrift in *your* county government." And it (the thrift) must be so. After all, all your expensive ads and extensive speeches do so indicate.

Unfortunately, but a few days before the election (for which the voter turnout is anticipated to be so great it will set a record), the media breaks the story concerning the several unexplained — but expensive — junkets you, your staff, and your family (and not a few of your friends and supporters) made to, among other interesting destinations, Las Vegas, New York, Atlanta, Los Angeles, Atlantic City, Reno, San Francisco, Miami Beach, San Juan, New Orleans, and Gary, Indiana. You can explain away the others; but Gary presents somewhat of a challenge.

And challenged you are . . . by your crusading opponent, at the debate — the debate educational television decided to televise nationally, live, as an example of civics in action for the youth of the country.

OK; you silver-tongued devil, **what are you gonna say?**

- [ ] "We're trying to attract industry to the county."
- [ ] "I guess we took the wrong exit on the interstate."
- [ ] "We were trying to broaden our tax base."
- [ ] "I didn't realize we had gone that far."
- [ ] "I thought it was deductible."
- [ ] "Travel is broadening."
- [ ] "My grandmother died again."
- [ ] "The frequent flyer miles will lower our travel expenses in the future."
- [ ] "I was trying to teach my children some geography."
- [ ] "Staff education and development is critical to good county government."
- [ ] "The devil made me do it."
- [ ] "My chief of staff has trouble reading a map."
- [ ] "After Gary, there was just no stopping."

THE DEVIL MADE ME DO IT!

All Things Being EQ

Select the most appropriate excuse for each sticky situation.

1. You are the admininistrator in the county assessor's office. A very, very concerned citizen calls to inquire why the assessed value of his house (last year's assessed value, $140,000) is now $450,000. I'm also curious.
   a. We have a new assessment technique, a new assessor . . . and a new computer system.
   b. The new administration is cutting out all the waste in county government.
   c. Just kidding, just kidding.
   d. Hello? Hello? We must have a bad connection.

2. You are the elected official in the part of the city known as "The pothole capital of the world." A citizen, whose car badly needs a realignment, asks you why your jurisdiction has such a well-deserved potholier-than-thou reputation. Speak, oh wise elected official.
   a. I had a committee study that particular problem.
   b. The previous incumbent (from the other party) planned it.
   c. Your car must be out of alignment .
   d. We've had a lot of (hot, cold, wet, dry — choose carefully, taking into account current conditions) weather lately.

3. You are asked by an office buddy to put up an election sign in your front yard for a candidate for whom not only are you not going to vote, but for whose total defeat you are going to work. You decline. Your buddy, whose feelings you would prefer not to hurt, asks you why. Well?
   a. Our zoning prohibits the putting up of signs of any kind.
   b. I only recently embraced anarchy as the form of government of my choice.
   c. We already have the kids' lemonade stand in our front yard.
   d. I just had my lawn paved over.

4. The widely circulated and publicized city ordinance notwithstanding, your dog has just fouled the footpath. An irate neighbor, and the accompanying police officer, inquire as to how such an infraction of the law could come about. They have your attention.
   a. My dog is participating in a federal experiment.
   b. We were on our way to the vet about just that problem.
   c. We've had a lot of (hot, cold, wet, dry — choose carefully, taking into account current conditions) weather lately.
   d. No argument; but aren't you glad I gave away the elephant?

Scoring and Interpreting
   Correct answers are presented on page 89. How did you do?

Got A Match?

Match each sticky situation with the most appropriate excuse.
Sticky Situations

___A. During your latest IRS audit, you are asked about a series of particularly creative deductions. I'm waiting.

___B. The only appointed person on your office staff (interestingly enough your brother-in-law) is convicted of embezzling funds from the citizens. The prosecuting attorney inquires.

___C. You are going the wrong way on a one-way street. The officer who finally stops you has a real interest in why you would do such a thing.

___D. You are going the wrong way on a one-way street. The officer who finally stops you has a real interest in why you would do such a thing.

__E. You are dismissed from the police academy for stealing police academy graduation certificates.   Your mentors are curious.

Appropriate Excuses
__1. I didn't realize I had a brother-in-law.
__2. I'm putting my brother-in-law through accounting school.
__3. I'm just a sentimental fool who believes it takes a thief to catch a thief.
__4. Yes, but I was only going one way.
__5. Yes, but I was going in reverse.

Scoring and Interpreting
   Correct answers are presented on page 89. How did you do?

The Write Stuff

   Well citizen, regarding **the write stuff,** how do you plead?
   However you plead, please plead it pleasingly — and promptly — with the EXCUSE-O-GRAM provided by the court.
   Episode dismissed.
   Next episode.

SPORTS
These are not my shoes

Anyone who has participated in sports competition, watched sports competition, and/or known anyone from either of the first two categories knows winners tell jokes and losers yell deal . . . or offer excuses.

Deal?

Deal!

ATTENTION, GOLFERS *(real and/or imagined)*— you find yourself in the following sticky situation:

You are playing in a local, and prestigious, golf tournament.

Anyone who is anyone in the local golfing community is either playing or watching. The partner with whom you have been saddled is a notoriously particularly poor putter. You expect nothing from him . . . and so far he has not let you down . . . consistently.

Notwithstanding, you and your saddle lead the field by a single stroke. On the 17th hole (next-to-the-last hole, for you fortunate enough not to know), he misses an easy seven-inch attempt . . . badly. You are now tied, and indeed you are fit to so be.

Ever under control, you pick yourself — and your clubs — off the ground, get in his face, and proceed to instruct him loudly and publicly on the finer points of putting.

Fortunately, on the last hole (the 18th hole, for you fortunate enough not to know), *you* have a delightfully embarrassingly easy two-inch attempt, the making of which will retain the tie. As your putt rolls by the hole, and continues to roll, your partner (you remember, your former student at the 17th hole) casually wonders aloud (very, very, aloud) what your problem might be.

OK, potentially partially perplexed professional putter, you're up. **What are you gonna say?**

☐ "These are not my shoes."
☐ "The sun got in my eyes."
☐ "Damn fire ants!"
☐ "One of the spectators coughed."
☐ "I'm upset about worsening conditions in *(fill in world problem spot)*."
☐ "There ought to be a dress code for spectators."
☐ "My grandmother died again."
☐ "I'm used to artificial turf."
☐ "I'm used to real grass."
☐ "This toothache is killing me."
☐ "Didn't you feel the tremor?"
☐ "The shadows got in my eyes."
☐ "Did you see that?"
☐ "My great uncle suffered from the same nervous disorder, but he lived well into his thirties."
☐ "I was distracted by a flight of migrating birds."

DAMN FIRE ANTS

ATTENTION, BOWLERS — you find yourself in the following sticky situation:

As captain of your team, you are appropriately — not to mention vociferously and publicly — proud of what you and "the supporting people" (as you cleverly describe the other four nameless and faceless people to the media) have accomplished. In *the* national tournament, your team has a lead pipe cinch opportunity to win.

All that is required is for the last bowler on your team to knock down one or more pins on the final ball. What a break (as opposed to split)! *You* are the person with that opportunity. No problem! . . . and never mind the screaming fans and network TV.

You calmly and confidently step up and in and proceed to set some sort of international record for shortest distance between ball release and gutter entry. In the ensuing melee, many, many, people — to include that pushy network TV guy — call upon you to explain.

OK, gritty gutsy game gutter getter, you're up once again. **What are you gonna say?**

☐ "The sun got in my eyes."

☐ "These aren't my socks."

☐ "The pins are not regulation weight and size."

☐ "I had trouble finding a parking place."

☐ "What a warp!"

☐ "Someone in the gallery coughed."

☐ "I'm not used to these narrow lanes."

☐ "My grandmother died again."

☐ "An unexpectedly opened door caused a vacuum which in turn
   caused a sudden gust of wind which in turn affected the path
   of the ball."

☐ "These are not my shoes."

All Things Being EQ

As before, **select the most appropriate excuse for each sticky situation.**

1. You are the first baseman who drops the throw that should have ended the game. When asked why, what is your reply?
   - a. This is not my glove.
   - b. I thought I heard the national anthem being played, and I started to come to attention.
   - c. The infielder who threw me the ball threw a knuckler.
   - d. There ought to be a dress code for spectators.

2. After assuring your spouse it is not necessary to prepare dinner (because you will bring home enough fish for the next two nights), you arrive home having caught only a cold. When asked why, what is your reply?
   - a. There is a strange new limit on the number of fish you can catch.
   - b. On the way home, I was robbed by an international band of fish thieves.
   - c. The cat ate it, (pause) but . . .
   - d. Civility and sportsmanship (to say nothing of the game warden), demanded I throw them back.

3. You are dunking the basketball at the gun for what should be the winning basket. As the ball bounds past midcourt after hitting the heel of the basket, your understanding coach inquires why that might be. What is your reply?
   - a. I have never seen such live rims.
   - b. The rims are not regulation height.
   - c. The referee got in my way.
   - d. I was trying to set up the trailer.

4. You are the center on an NFL football team. Your snap for the game-winning field goal has just set a new distance (and height) record. The press — not to mention the coach, team, and fans — query you as to how this could be. What is your reply?
   a. I just can't seem to get used to these bifocals.
   b. Someone in the crowd coughed.
   c. The ball was under-inflated . . . *and* non-regulation.
   d. I thought the holder was taller.

Scoring and Interpretation
   Correct answers are on page 91. How was your performance? Oh really, why?

Got A Match?

Match each sticky situation with the most appropriate excuse.
Sticky Situations
___A. The easy ground ball goes cleanly through your legs. The manager asks you why.

___B. After knocking down all but one of the hurdles in the race you were supposed to dominate, the coach expresses interest.

___C. What would have been the winning touchdown pass slowly slips from your hands to the ground. Many people, all extremely irate, inquire.

___D. Although a 40 to 1 favorite, you are knocked out in the first thirty seconds of the first round. A lot of people — to include the boxing commissioner — ask why.

___E. Although the game ended at 4:00, and the stadium is but an hour away, you stagger in at about 9:15 (but at least the same day). Your spouse inquires.

Appropriate Excuses

__1. My breakfast was late . . . and over-cooked.

__2. I thought I was shorter.

__3. There can be little or no doubt I probably over-trained.

__4. I thought everyone knew I was the decoy.

__5. There was a delightful impromptu charity art exhibit after the game.

Scoring And Interpreting

This time the correct answers are on page 91. How did you do?

The Write Stuff

. . . and finally, as the clock and the episode run out, regarding **the write stuff,** OK, sport(s), do your thing — on page 80.

Let's win this one for the Excuser.

HOSPITALITY and TRAVEL
The kitchen is a little slow tonight

My first wife and I were at a really elegant restaurant recently; and . . .

Oh, I see. No, hold on. Before anyone — especially my first wife — gets upset, let me at least partially explain about my first wife and/or me — as well as our marriage.

So far at least, we have each had sixteen extremely happy years of marriage . . . unfortunately, not the same sixteen years.

This year (August 10th again, as I recall) we go for the tie-breaker . . . unless she forgets our anniversary again — in which case she had better have a great excuse.

Come to think of it, I kinda hope she *does* forget it again. I can use the excuse more than I can use her traditional anniversary gift. After all, how many pairs of brown socks can one man wear at one time?

What a thoughtful anniversary gift (again this year), Dear. Thank you. I wish my gift for you had arrived in time for this eventful occasion (or is it occasional event?), but . . .

Incidentally, I don't know how it is in your marriage; but in our marriage, *I* always get the last word . . . even if that word is "Yesdear."

Anyway, as I was saying before I was so rudely interrupted, my first wife and I were at a really elegant restaurant recently; and, given the less than generous table spacing, we couldn't help overhearing the conversation between the waitron and the guests at the next table.

The guests asked the waitron for a recommendation. To which the waitron replied, "Another restaurant."

So much for organizational commitment.

Actually, I should have suspected something was amiss at the restaurant when the host's reply to my question about the availability of a non-smoking section was, "No, but we do have a large, and we think ample, non-spitting section," for which I immediately opted — over my first wife's protestations. (I told you it was a really elegant restaurant.)

We're going back . . . often — at least on our anniversary this year (which, as I recall, is May 3rd) . . . but only if I can get a table in the non-talking section.

ATTENTION, DESK CLERKS AND OTHER HOSTS OF WEARY TRAVELERS, CONVENTIONEERS, AND ASSORTED (OR SORDID) ROAD WARRIORS — you find yourself in the following sticky situation:

It is your first day on the job as director of reservations and check-in at the hotel. It has been a really tough day already (and you've only been on the job for ten minutes).

However, to your (unlimited) credit, you did do an excellent job of handling the large convention of The Association of Bagpipers of North America, who, for some reason, showed up two days earlier than anyone expected (but that's OK; they'll be staying three days longer than anyone expected). Oh, sure, some might question your judgment about putting them on the same floor with all those folks from the American Association of Teachers of Classical Music; but hey, that's why they put you in charge.

Things seem to be working out . . . finally. The property is now at — or maybe just beyond, if you count the people you put in sleeping bags in the small banquet room — capacity.

Nothing to do now except wait for your relief to show up, about a few hours hence. But before hence comes about, here comes a bus carrying a tour group of world class champion professional wrestlers (many showered) with no more than twenty extremely well-muscled would-be guests . . . would-be guests only because they claim to have reservations . . . which comes as a total surprise to you . . . and all your records.

Did I mention you were the only one on duty?

OK, deft daring durable desk director, you're up. **What are you gonna say?** (. . . and I really recommend you talk fast, as several of the larger — but less reasonable — wrestlers are stripping down to their tights.)

☐ "I'm new on the job."

☐ "Your rooms aren't quite ready."

☐ "I'm sorry; I don't speak (perhaps English)."

☐ "There is a taxidermists' strike."

☐ "We're expecting an emergency."

☐ "I'll have to check with ('housekeeping' is always good)."

☐ "My grandmother died again."

☐ "Our computer made an error."

☐ "I can't check you in without proof of age."

☐ "The person in charge is out to lunch . . . and isn't expected back until after I get off duty . . . in a few hours."

☐ "We don't accept that credit card."

☐ "I don't work here (anymore)."

I'LL HAVE TO CHECK WITH HOUSEKEEPING

ATTENTION, GOURMET AND/OR GOURMAND DINERS — you find yourself in the following sticky situation:

Not unlike any other minor major city, your city has one particularly elegant (some might even say snooty) — and terribly expensive — restaurant so popular not only are reservations necessary, but so hard to get you have to call an unlisted number ahead to *make* a reservation just to call *for* a reservation.

Just to be seen there is a high water (imported, definitely not domestic) mark of the season in terms of upward social mobility. And the food is rumored to be good, too.

Be that as it may (or mayn't, as the case may — or mayn't — be), your extremely significant other has dropped hints regarding her desire to be seen there . . . even to eat there.

Somehow, you do it. Not only do you break through the reservation barrier, but you passionately request and do in fact obtain *the* restaurant's most romantic corner booth. Never mind the financial consideration to the host with which you were forced to part. The important thing is your self-humiliation has paid off with *the* reservation at *the* restaurant. Whether or not you are shunted off to the bar for an hour (two, tops) is beside the point.

Your good intentions vis-a-vis *the* restaurant notwithstanding, you arrive an hour late for the cherished reservation. Wishing you had gone to an equally elegant place with a drive-thru option, you elbow your way past the folks — *all* the folks, especially the ones who seem most angry about waiting — in (or is it on? I never get that right!) line.

As you finally get to the host, he inquires as to why you might be so late for the reservation.

All eyes, ears (noses and throats), and growling stomachs lock on to you. It suddenly occurs to you John Milton may have had it all wrong, . . . perhaps they also wait who stand and serve.

OK, genuinely glaringly gratuitous gourmet and/or gourmand, I'm curious; how *are* you going to soothe the savage beast? **What are you gonna say?**

- ☐ "My watch stopped."
- ☐ "The interview with (whoever is the current fad) ran late."
- ☐ "There were complications in surgery."
- ☐ "The plane was late."
- ☐ "The ox was late."
- ☐ "We were held hostage in a bank robbery."
- ☐ "The cat and the dog threw up."
- ☐ "My grandmother died again."
- ☐ "It's *her* birthday."
- ☐ "I'm coming from a different time zone."
- ☐ "When was the time change?"
- ☐ "We were kidnapped . . . *twice* . . . but escaped."
- ☐ "We had a flat tire."
- ☐ "We didn't realize you had moved ."
- ☐ "I wanted to give the wine a chance to breathe."

I WANTED TO GIVE THE WINE A CHANCE TO BREATHE

All Things Being EQ

Select the most appropriate excuse for each sticky situation.

1. You are the individual at the airlines who is responsible for the delivery of luggage. Although you are located in Chicago, you get a call from a passenger in San Diego who casually wonders if you know where in the wherever his luggage might be — and how such a thing could happen. OK, completely culpable common carrier, what is your reply?
   a. The computer is down . . . again.
   b. Hello? Hello? We must have a bad connection.
   c. There is a front moving through New England.
   d. We're shaking the bugs out of a new system.

2. Your credit card people call you and casually inquire why your last month's payment has not been received. Shocked and indignant (but not really surprised), what is your snappy comeback?
   a. The check is in the mail. (There, feel better?)
   b. I hope you people haven't lost it . . . again.
   c. Could it have been on that ship that sank off the coast of Mexico last week?
   d. The fax is in the mail.

3. A guest in the hotel calls to complain to you, the assistant manager, about the room being dirty, the toilet not working, the party next door being out of hand, and the pay television running amok. Sincere inquiry is made as to what you are going to do about it. Well?
   a. Hello? Hello? We must have a bad connection.
   b. We've been working on it all day.
   c. I'll call Housekeeping . . . *and* Security.
   d. We've just struck an iceberg.

4. You are the waitron of choice. Notwithstanding, it has been almost an hour since you took the guests' orders and passed said orders on to the chef (you're pretty sure). Flagging you down, the increasingly emaciated guests register their displeasure. What is your pleasure?

    a. I thought you might like to linger over your drinks.

    b. You really can't rush classic American cooking.

    c. We age our own beef.

    d. The kitchen is a little slow tonight.

Scoring And Interpreting

    As in times (or episodes) gone by, generate and evaluate your EQ score. The correct responses appear on page 91.

Got A Match?

Match each sticky situation with the most appropriate excuse. . . . or vice versa, whichever comes second.

Sticky Situations

__ A. A regular dinner guest at your restaurant, with a reservation, shows up promptly; but the table is not available. The word why comes to mind . . . and to you.

__ B. As you check out of your hotel room, which looks suspiciously as if one of the decisive battles of World War II had only recently been fought there, the manager expresses more than idle curiosity. And?

__ C. You are the check-out clerk at the motel. The guest's bill seems to be $9,000 more than he estimated. A real stickler, he inquires of you. Yes?

___D. There is something floating on top of the guest's not-so-clear consommé. Ever the entomologist, he inquires (in Latin, at least at first). May I have the check and your reply, please?

___E. Although your client distinctly remembers telling you, the travel agent, she wanted to fly to London, her ticket does indeed read Omaha. She expresses a certain amount of dissatisfaction . . . and disorientation. May I hear your excuse itinerary, please?

Appropriate Excuses
___1. It must be a slight glitch at corporate headquarters
___2. The chef is pushing out the envelope of creativity.
___3. We're still cleaning up from the gangland hit earlier in the evening.
___4. Who were those people involved in that riot?
___5. I thought the change of pace would be appealing to you.

Scoring And Interpreting
Again, generate and evaluate your EQ score. Correct responses are presented on page 91. How did you make out this time? Too bad, checkout time is rapidly approaching. How *do* you account for your score?

The Write Stuff

In terms of **the write stuff,** if there is no stationery in your room, either call Housekeeping (or Security) or use the EXCUSE-O-GRAM provided. Incidentally, why *isn't* there any stationery in your room?

ALL-PURPOSE COMEBACKS
FOR WHEN NOT LISTENING
There's a lot of that going around

Has it ever happened to you? You know, you're engaged (sorta) in conversation, but you're really not listening (I said, you're really not listening . . . thinking perhaps of . . . well, whatever).

And then, all too suddenly, you are snapped back to reality when the other party in the so-called conversation pauses and makes eye contact — clearly inviting you to become a more active participant in the social interaction.

Whoops! If only you had been listening.

Perhaps you could have contributed something genuinely pithy. . . or even clever and/or important. At least you could have saved the relationship you valued . . . valued, but not enough to listen.

On the other hand, as they used to ask in one of the homemaker magazines, can this relationship be saved? You bet your farm and/or your whatever it can be saved . . . and fairly easily at that. Read on.

All you have to do is toss in (or is it out? I never get that right!) one of those expressions everyone values — even though the expression itself is just a tad less than of any value. *You* know what I'm talking about. We've *all* done it.

Rich, heavy, insightful stuff of which nothing is made (and remade) . . . platitudes gone platinum . . . stuff like:

☐ "They just don't make them like they used to."
☐ "Oh, my."
☐ "The story of my life."
☐ "I certainly hope so."
☐ "Hmmmm."
☐ "Things are tough all over."
☐ "Oh yeah?" (a particularly compelling crusher)
☐ "Have I ever lied to you before?"
☐ "Don't you just love it?"
☐ "Just lucky, I guess."
☐ "Tell me about it."
☐ . . . or even, "Hey, tell me about it."

If you have never engaged in such face (or the other end) saving behavior, you are unique.

When our son was active in the Boy Scouts (and he sure was, eventually achieving Eagle status — Josh, clean up your nest), we were appropriately supportive and involved.
Tell me about it. . . . or even, Hey, tell me about it.
On more than one occasion, I found myself at meetings and other social interactions where I was engaged (sorta) in this conversation (sorta) with people (sorta) with whom I really, really, had nothing in common except (1) our sons were members of the same Scout troop, (2) they too were appropriately supportive and involved, and (3) we were in this conversation (sorta).

I readily confess not always being as attentive as I should have been. But I did make two keen observations — both of which led to a critical insight.

FIRST KEEN OBSERVATION: I noticed, regardless of the positive or negative nature of the critical incident described, e.g., "The boys had a wonderful trip to Philmont," or "All the equipment was lost," or "All the food was spoiled," or "The county really appreciated their effort," or "It rained the whole time," or "There was a 300 percent cost overrun," or whatever, the super sage comment *someone* in the conversational group always would make was:

"HEY, THAT'S WHAT SCOUTING IS ALL ABOUT."

. . . at which point the balance of the group would simultaneously smile (knowingly, I guess) and nod their respective heads (equally knowingly, I guess).

SECOND KEEN OBSERVATION: I figured, if I could be the one to make the "HEY, THAT'S WHAT SCOUTING IS ALL ABOUT" comment, I could not only fit in better, but—pay attention—I could be even less attentive.

. . . and, no surprise, it worked (Almost too well). Soon the other parents were nominating me for all sorts of responsibilities because of their perception of me as a person who *really* understood what . . .

Fortunately I had a few excuses up my merit badge. Anyway, regarding the critical insight . . .

CRITICAL INSIGHT: It finally occurred to me this social verbal gambit was *the* general model and *the* comeback for *all* forms of *the* sticky situation described in this episode.

And that is (are you ready for this?), all you have to do when that conversational pause comes (and it *will*); and the others look at (and to) you for some super sage contribution, is to spew forth:

"HEY, THAT'S WHAT *(whatever the topic —* ***that*** *much attention must be paid)* **IS ALL ABOUT."**

It works every time. Trust me on this one.

Hey, that's what this episode is all about.

ATTENTION, HUMAN BEINGS — you find yourself once again in one of those situations (actually, *that* situation) I was describing above . . . the one in which *you were not listening* (I said the one in which *you were not listening*).

It's the classic situation; I don't think I can (or will even attempt to) improve on it. So here it is one more time . . . probably for the last time.

You are semi-disengaged in conversation with this other person. The other person pauses, seemingly suggesting it is your turn to say *something*. You suddenly wish, really wish, you had been listening. Go ahead. It's your turn; and we're all waiting to hear what you have to say — and you do *have* to say *something*!

OK, learned lax lethargic lackadaisical listener, you're up. **What are you gonna say?**

☐ "How quickly they forget."

☐ "Hey, I can handle that."

☐ "Alone at last."

☐ "Hey, that's show business."

☐ "I thought they would never leave."

☐ "Hey, I can deal with that."

☐ "OK; but you'll never be invited back."

☐ "How droll."

☐ "How wonderfully droll!"

☐ "Close enough."

HEY, THAT'S WHAT IT'S ALL ABOUT

- [ ] "Worked out just right."
- [ ] "Well, I guess we showed them."
- [ ] "About a buck and a half an hour."
- [ ] "Hey, that's what (you pick it) is all about."
- [ ] "Just lucky I guess."
- [ ] "You think that's easy?"
- [ ] "I may be crazy, but I'm not stupid."
- [ ] "I may be stupid, but I'm not crazy."
- [ ] "I would have done *(or said)* the same thing in your place."
- [ ] "Listen."
- [ ] "Who cares?"
- [ ] ". . . and that's the good news!"
- [ ] "You did what?"
- [ ] "You said what?"
- [ ] "That good?"
- [ ] "That good!"
- [ ] "That good."
- [ ] "He *(or she)* loved it — right?"
- [ ] "That's hard to believe."
- [ ] "You can't be serious."
- [ ] "You gotta love it."
- [ ] "Hey, he's *(or she's)* the boss *(or dean)*."
- [ ] "There's a lot of that going around."

Announced Pop Quiz

Select the most appropriate comeback for each sticky situation.

1. You are semi-disengaged in conversation with this other person. The other person pauses, seemingly suggesting it is your turn to say *something*. You suddenly wish, really wish, you had been listening. Go ahead. It's your turn; and we're all waiting to hear what you have to say — and you *do have* to say *something!*
   - a. Maybe he (or she) won't notice.
   - b. Include me out.
   - c. A regular (John Wayne or Bob Hope often works well here).
   - d. Who listens?

2. (See sticky situation 1 above.)
   - a. And then it got bad!
   - b. Life goes on.
   - c. What's the good news?
   - d. It doesn't get any better (or worse) than that.

3. (See sticky situation 4 below.)
   - a. It's a great life if you don't weaken.
   - b. And then it got good!
   - c. Tell me about it!
   - d. So much for one trial learning!

4. (See sticky situation 3 above.)
   - a. Hey, nobody's perfect.
   - b. Whatever .
   - c. Beats me.
   - d. Hey, that's what (you pick it) is all about.

Correct answers appear on page 92.   Interpretation remains unchanged.

When The Time Is Right

Match each sticky situation with the most appropriate comeback.
Sticky Situations
A. You are semi-disengaged in conversation with this other person. The other person pauses, seemingly suggesting it is your turn to say *something*. You suddenly wish, really wish, you had been listening. Go ahead. It's your turn; and we're all waiting to hear what you have to say — and you do *have to* say *something!*

___B. (See sticky situation A above.)

___C. (See sticky situation E below.)

___D. (See sticky situation B above.)

___E. (See sticky situation C above.)

Appropriate Comebacks
___1. That's the way it goes.
___2. Isn't that always the way of it?
___3. Easy come, easy go.
___4. Sometimes you win; and sometimes you lose (and sometimes you don't even get in the game).
___5. And you thought I was just another pretty face.

Correct answers appear (apparently) on page 92. Interpretation is as before.

The Write Stuff

Regarding **the write stuff,** if you're listening (I said . . .), use of the EXCUSE-O-GRAM is recommended. Hey, that's what this episode is all about (and there's a lot of that going around).

Y'know, I suppose I really should get around to that procrastination episode, but . . .

PROCRASTINATION
Here's looking at you, Scarlett

How to begin? *Where* to begin? When to begin?
. . . but not *if* to begin. Actually, I really should have done this sooner.

I am *really* at home (read expert) regarding procrastination — as I will demonstrate eventually . . . unless something (anything!) else comes up.
. . . and speaking of home, you will have no trouble recognizing my home. It is the one with all the extremely well-sharpened pencils.
Procrastination (I even love the *sound* of the word; it sounds positively obscene) is really the highest form of the noble art of excuses. Just think about the concept (*now* . . . not later!) . . . devoting your waking hours to coming up with explanations and/or reasons with which to convince *yourself*. Can one aspire to anything higher?

I readily confess to being a procrastinator — and right here and right now!
However, unlike so many, I am a *conscientious* procrastinator. That is, just as soon as I know I have to do something, I *immediately* begin putting it off. (Don't take my word for it; check with my editor).
And being so introspective, I knew I needed professional help for this delightfully lingering condition. Our family physician suggested I join the local chapter (or is it episode?) of Procrastinators Anonymous.

Why not? I had been meaning to do it for years anyway.

I did finally join PA; and it's great. I don't understand why I didn't do it sooner. What really impressed me about the group was the spring meeting was in October . . . late October.

In all semi-honesty, it hasn't changed my behavior any; but, compared to the other PA members, I look positively compulsive.

Actually, so far I haven't done much more than stand up and say "My name is (my name); and I am a procrastinator." But there are lots of great things to do with the group . . . when we get around to it.

For example, our annual field trip this year will be to visit a glacier (which reminds me . . . I need to pack). I can't wait to try my fast film with the stop action feature on my camera . . . just as soon as I take it out of the box.

And regarding the annual time changes, we haven't re-set our PA clock (which, not so incidentally, has twenty-five hours on it . . . and runs very slowly) but I'm sure we will . . . eventually.

I'm serving on the planning committee. So far we haven't done much but we have plans . . . lots of plans. Our motto is "First Things Third."

We go to restaurants without reservations and don't mind the wait. We look forward to sitting in waiting rooms, we even have a list of the ten best waiting rooms in town . . . with a special category for dental offices.

We sit around not opening gifts . . . and other mail.

We're considering getting a chapter mascot . . . maybe a sloth . . . but not right away.

And to take an historical perspective (we love history), Benjamin Franklin might have known about dime stores, mints, and other such stuff; but he didn't know shucks (thanks, Mr. Clemens, I needed that) about procrastination. Why do today what you can put off until tomorrow? . . . or, better yet, the day after tomorrow? After all, tomorrow *is* another day! (and frankly, my dear, I do . . . but not now, I have an episode to write).

ATTENTION — you find yourself in the following sticky situation:

Heeding my advice, you rush (yecch!) out and join *your* local episode (or is it chapter) of Procrastinators Anonymous. When you fail to attend your very first PA meeting, the membership is so positively impressed the nominations committee immediately calls an unprecedented emergency meeting — the immediate (equally unprecedented) result of which is your unanimous nomination for the presidency. The equally impressed membership immediately (wow!) goes along . . . by acclamation.

All that remains is for you to prepare your acceptance speech . . . not due for a whole week.

As the days flit by, as you stare at that fully loaded and ready-to-explode word processor, and as your well meaning but obviously non-understanding spouse, children, and friends take turns asking you *when* you are going to prepare your acceptance speech, what thoughts stray across your mind?

. . . all of which is just one more way to say OK, perennially professional procrastinating person, you're up. **What are you gonna say (to yourself)?**

> ☐ "I'll think about it tomorrow."
> ☐ "What's the rush?"
> ☐ "It will keep."
> ☐ "I'm thirsty."
> ☐ "A few sharp pencils couldn't hurt."
> ☐ "Today would be a good day to clean up the (   )."
> ☐ "Did I just hear a pin drop?"
> ☐ "There's plenty of time."

☐ "I had better change the batteries in my (   )."

☐ "How long has it been since I've seen a dentist anyway?"

☐ "The lawn needs edging."

☐ "My toenails need clipping."

☐ "With that electrical storm threatening, perhaps I should turn off the word processor."

☐ "Haste makes waste."

☐ "If I leave for services now, perhaps I can get a good seat."

☐ "Isn't tonight the night the cable weather channel is going to be showing reruns of all the good weather of 1934?"

☐ "I really should shop for that anniversary gift."

☐ "I really should shop for that birthday gift."

☐ "I really should write that check for the alumni association."

☐ "I really should write that term paper."

☐ "I really should clean up my room."

☐ "I really should have that talk with my child about reproduction."

☐ "I really should go visit (   ) in the hospital."

☐ "I've been meaning to pick up *Gone With the Wind* again for the longest time." And after all . . .

☐ "Tomorrow *is* another day."

Announced Pop Quiz (All Things Being EQ)

Select the most appropriate (self) excuse for each sticky situation.

1. Procrastinators Anonymous was so impressed with your introspection they have offered you the presidency for *life*. Now they're waiting (patiently) for your answer. Well, they're still waiting.
    a. I need to check my calendar.
    b. I'll get back to you.
    c. Let me check the TV listings.
    d. Just as soon as I finish reading *Gone With The Wind* . . . again.

2. You have been meaning to clean up that mess downstairs. Your spouse has also been meaning for you to clean up that mess downstairs. You are again considering it. Let me hear it.
    a. Next (   )day.
    b. Who would notice anyway?
    c. If I'm not mistaken, this month has an "r" in it.
    d. What if I find something important down there?

3. Everyone agrees. A will *does* seem in order. Why not?
    a. It's bad luck to even think about such things; I once heard of a guy who . . .
    b. Who, me?
    c. It can wait.
    d. Perhaps after the spring thaw.

4. The manuscript is due to the editor Friday. What is your thinking?
    a. I could use a few good erasers to go with all these sharpened pencils.
    b. Today is only Tuesday.
    c. Today is only Wednesday.
    d. Today is only Thursday.

It would be presumptuous of me to think I could give *you* the correct answers this time. No, this time you will just have to do your own scoring. Talk about the honor system! It's time for you to solo. . . by yourself.

However, I do not choose to abdicate my responsibility regarding interpretation of your self-evaluated self-performance.

The norms and their interpretation are unchanged. *Gotcha!*

When The Time Is Right (Got A Match?)

Match each sticky situation with the most appropriate (self) excuse.

Sticky Situations

___A. The time really, I mean really, has come for you to tell the people in the apartment next door about the volume on their sound system. Share your thought(s).

___B. That toothache just won't go away. What do you think?

___C. There it is again — that rattle in your car. Well?

___D. The bully next door keeps picking on your child. Perhaps the time has come to confront the bully's parent . . . the big bully. And your position is?

___E. You have this insatiable urge to offer excuses to others, and you find yourself forever procrastinating. Any thoughts?

Appropriate (Self) Excuses

__1. Maybe it will stop.
__2. Maybe it will stop.
__3. Maybe it will stop.
__4. Maybe it will stop.
__5. Maybe it will stop.

Scoring and Interpreting

Once again, it would be presumptuous of me to think I could give you the correct answers. No, once again, you will just have to do your own scoring. Please make me look good.

Again however, I do not choose to abdicate my responsibility regarding interpretation of your self-evaluated self-performance. The norms and their intepretation remain unchanged. . . and you remain gotcha-ed!

The Excuse Institute of North America (and Georgia) — The Write Stuff

And for the last time, regarding **the write stuff,** if you get around to it, fill in — and return — the EXCUSE-O-GRAM. Don't put it (or me) off.

Well, I have to end this procrastination episode *right now* because my editor is beating down my door (with a big blunt blue pencil . . . which I would be pleased to sharpen) demanding this not-quite-overdue-yet manuscript . . . which I suppose I really should have done sooner.

But I successfully procrastinated by using the ultimate excuse . . . the one I have been saving for just the right moment. And I think now is just the right moment.

Oh, I'll get to it later . . . or maybe *next time*.

MAILER
Excuse-O-Gram

Do you have some sticky situations, excuses, comebacks, and procrastinations to contribute? (you gave *where?*) Here's your chance . . . literally.

Simply grasp pen and/or word processor between thumb and forefinger, complete and mail (that's important, otherwise . . .) the following EXCUSE-O-GRAM to:

Dr. Warren S. Blumenfeld
The Big **E**
The **E**xcuse Institute of North America (and Georgia)
International Worldwide Headquarters (Home Office)
P. O. Box 14413
Atlanta, Georgia 30324
Attention: Department **E**

Dear Big **E**:

For whatever reason (and please don't give me any excuses), the following sticky situations, excuses, comebacks, and procrastinations did *not* appear in MY GRAND-MOTHER DIED AGAIN *& Other Almost Believable Excuses.* Big **E**, this is inexcusable. I demand you include them in your next collection of excuses.

STICKY SITUATIONS   EXCUSES / COMEBACKS / PROCRASTINATIONS

_____

_____

_____

_____

_____

_____

_____

_____

_____

_____

Love,

Your Name *(correct spelling preferred)* _____

Your Address _____

Your shoe size *(watch the mail)* _____

P.S. I recommend you entitle your next collection of excuses _____

My favorite excuse was _____

My favorite comeback was _____

My favorite procrastination was _____

My favorite sticky situation was _____

80

ACKNOWLEDGMENTS
I would have included you by name, but. . .

This a self-help book — I'm trying to help myself. Additional acknowledgments follow.

In applied behavioral measurement and research (my area of expertise in real life — if indeed life is real), there is a data generation/collection technique called critical incident method. (That's really just applied behavioral science talk for collecting anecdotes.)

This book is essentially a collection of critical incidents . . . specifically those startling, i.e., critical, explanations people offer to account for their behavior — or misbehavior. It is a partial result of my dull, but stodgy, academic research — for years carried on casually and alone, then systematically and alone, and much more recently systematically and with the help of (temporarily, but, happily, not terminally) unhappy students who were made a little less unhappy by the happy task of collecting critical incidents involving excuses.

Some academic purists may think it more than unfortunate such originally academic research has turned out to be so humorous; but I have an excuse. As a matter of fact, I have a bookful of excuses — and this is it.

Said staid academic purists notwithstanding, I would like to acknowledge the following individuals for a variety of contributions —many of which were made intentionally:

A forever-to-be anonymous student . . . for the inadvertent contribution of the book's title.

And a goodly — and growing — number (too many to mention specifically, but they know who they are) of students, staff, faculty, and administrators at Georgia State University . . . for a number of things (also too many to mention specifically, but they know what they are).

And Steven Kutner, David Hein, Norman Sanders, and Herbert Kaufman . . . for keeping me in the game. And several people I have never met and whose names I will never know — two of whom are in my sight at all times . . . for their unique generosity.

And Woody Allen, Norman Arey, Ed Baker, Leslie Bayor, Ken Bernhardt, Al Bernie, David Black, Jack Blicksilver, Milton Blood, Devera Blumenfeld, Fagel Blumenfeld, Jack Blumenfeld, Mary Boyd, Billy Bowles, Shel Breskow, Mel Brooks, Herschel Brown, Mike Bucki, Bill Buel, Charley Burden, Bill Byham, Carey Bynum, George Carlin, Sandra Carnet, Dan Carson, Ginger Carter, Fred Cavinder, Lord Chesterfield, Tom Clark, Don Crane, Mike Dale, Beth Day, Lidia deLeon, Mark Donovan, Norville Downie, Laurie Edwards, Jean Feraca, Stan Firestone, John Flanagan, Joe Foerst, Lee Fowler, Kathy Gable, Joe Goodman, George Gordon, Jerry Granowsky, Burton Gruber, Lucy Hayes, Tom Higgins, Hillel, Max Holland, Adrienne Ingrum, Mike Jedel, Alix Kenagy, Bill Kent, Audree Koenigsberg, Kathy Landwehr, Rich Lederer, Bob Lee, Jackie Leonard, Larry Levin, Candy Magee, Julius Marx, J. P. McCarthy, Max McDaniel, Lynn McGill, Mike Mescon, Mike Miller, Ed Miles, Patrice Miles, Ron Mora, Pat Morrell, Kathi Mothershed, Sam Mudd, Don O'Briant, Ken Olshan, Robert Orben, Bill Osborn, John Palms, Linda Parker, Bob Perloff, Margaret Quinlin, Hermann Remmers, Lucille Richardson, Bernie Rimland, Jaine Rodack, Bill Rutherford, Ed Rundquist, Hugh Russell, Mort Sahl, Bob Scott, Cheryl Scott, Allison Shirreffs, Patti Shock, Max Shulman, Don Silverman, Faye Smallwood, Jill Smith, David Snell, Dick Snow, Bill Sone, Ron Sone, Charlie Storrs, Gerry Strand, James Taylor, Sherry Terrell, Morton Teicher, Susan Thurman, Cal Warlick, Ralph Wehunt, Jerry Weisbrodt, Martha Woodham, Steven Wright, Lillian Yeilding, Vickie York, Doug Young, and Henny Youngman . . . for a variety of reasons — related and unrelated.

And Josh Blumenfeld . . . for definitely *not* being one of those two people described on page viii (although occasionally he does come dangerously close) — but I love him anyway.

And Esther Blumenfeld . . . for understanding me, and this book, and excuses better (and more) than any rational person deserves — and about which understanding I am both extremely embarrassed and uncomfortable. (Your anniversary present, still coming from a long way away, is on its way, Dear. . . any day now.)

And finally (just when you thought it would never end, right?), family, friends, colleagues, strangers, and other imperfect people everywhere . . . for being so credibly human.

I would have included you by name, but . . .

WSB
Atlanta, Georgia
December 1990

About the author

Warren S. Blumenfeld, Ph.D., Dean of Oxymorons *and* Earl of Excuses, has traveled the world (well, he would have, but he got stuck in traffic) to catalog both the ordinary and the outlandish. He is also the author of two highly successful humor books on oxymorons, **JUMBO SHRIMP** and **PRETTY UGLY.** Dr. Blumenfeld writes a humor column for *The Atlanta Business Chronicle* and has been featured on over 300 radio and television talk shows as well as in *People* magazine.

Photograph by Kathryn Heath Gable

About the illustrator

Award-winning illustrator Cal Warlick is creative director for the *Gwinnett Daily News* and is also the illustrator of LeRoy Powell's **OUT OF MY HEAD,** Lynne Alpern and Esther Blumenfeld's **IN-LAWS, OUTLAWS *& Other Theories of Relativity,*** and Jerry Farber's **SEX, WEALTH & POWER,** all from Peachtree.